Sparkle Considers Children in Art

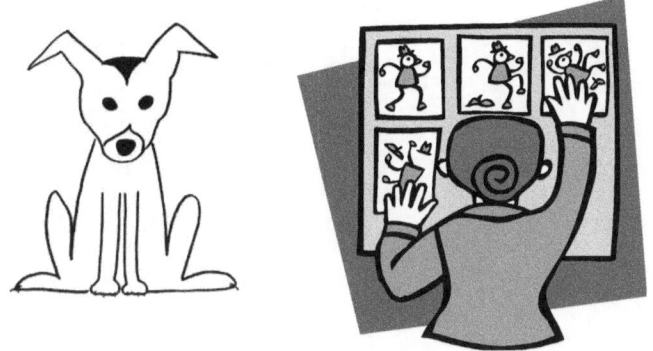

By Elizabeth Bixby

Dedicated to my sons, C.J
and Brody

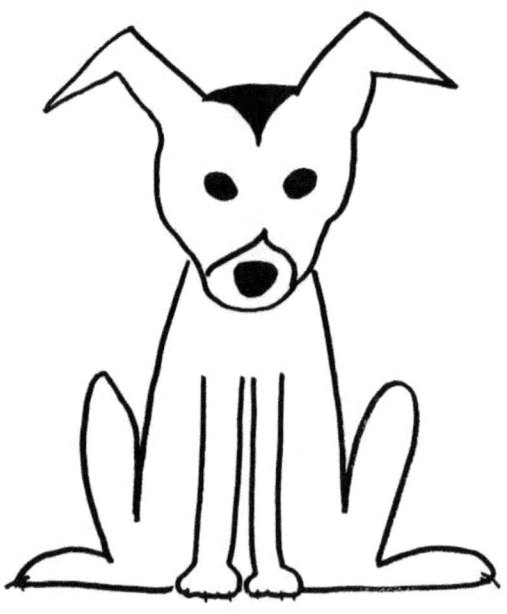

Hi! I'm Sparkle.

My mom is an artist.

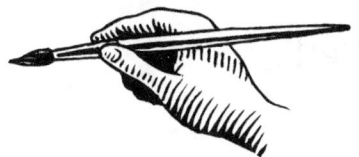

Even though I'm a pup, I consider myself a child of art.

Won't you be a child of art with me, and learn all we can about art?

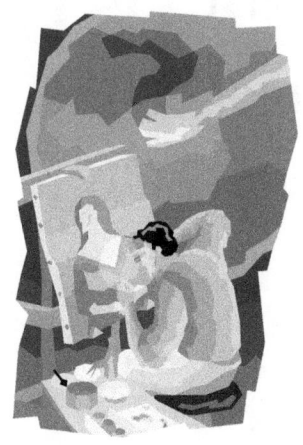

Let's learn about works of art about children.

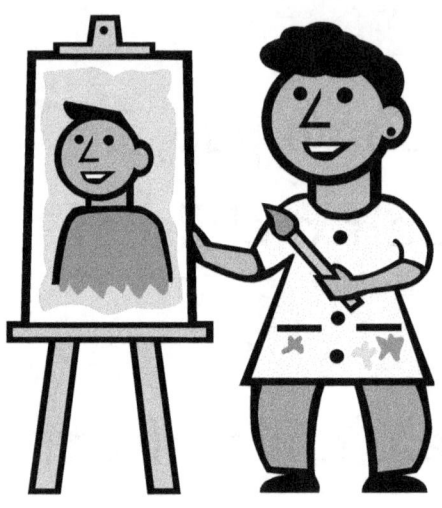

I really like art with children in it. It makes me feel happy.

Many artists throughout time have included children in fine art.

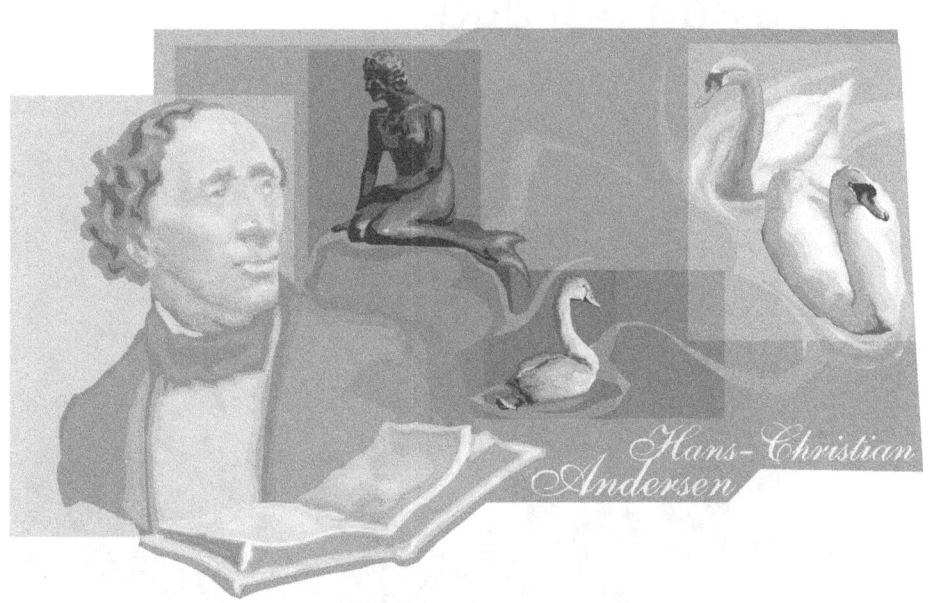

Artists added children to their paintings to represent time as well as to provide different proportions of sizes, as in Le Pont Neuf by Jean Beraud.

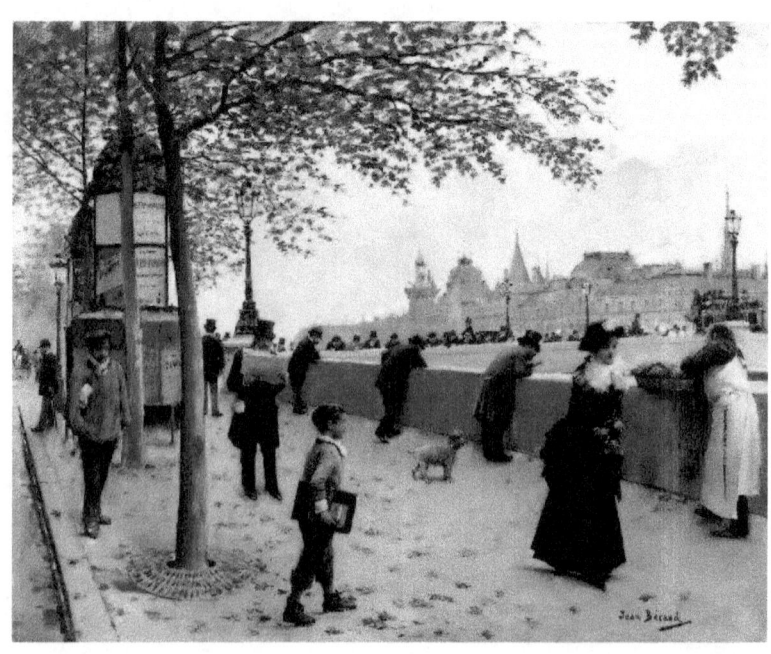

Artwork from ancient Roman times of children allows us a look into the past to see how children looked and lived then. This piece is a sculpture of a baby.

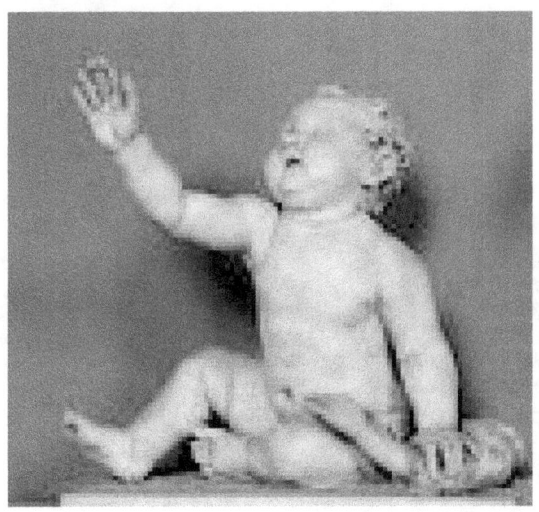

Art gives historians a real life glimpse or peek at real life. For instance, we know about King Tut from his tomb and the artwork made for and included with the child king.

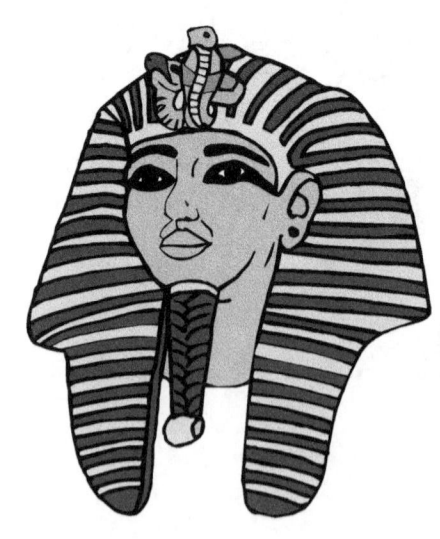

Medieval art often included children, also.

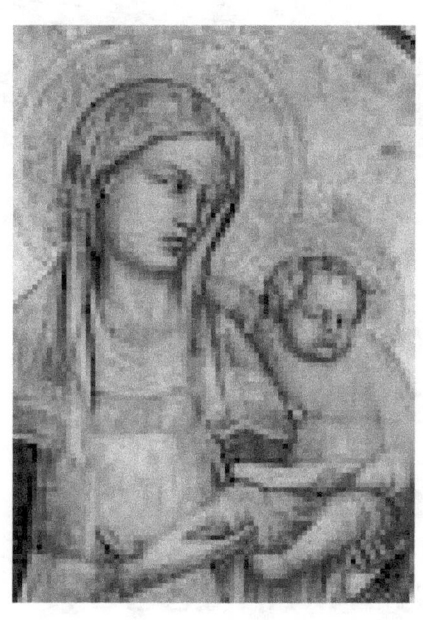

Art visually preserves history.

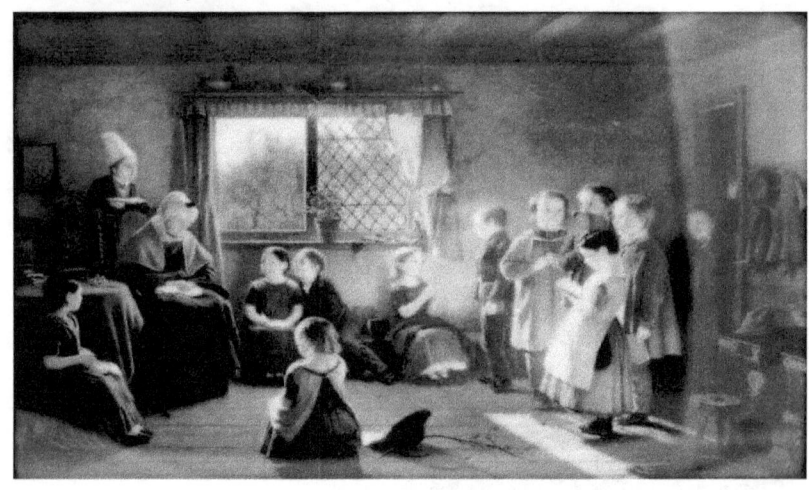

This painting, Victorian Country Classroom by Thomas Webster, shows a day in the life of an 1800's school. It looks quite different than today's classrooms.

There's a saying, "A picture is worth a thousand words."

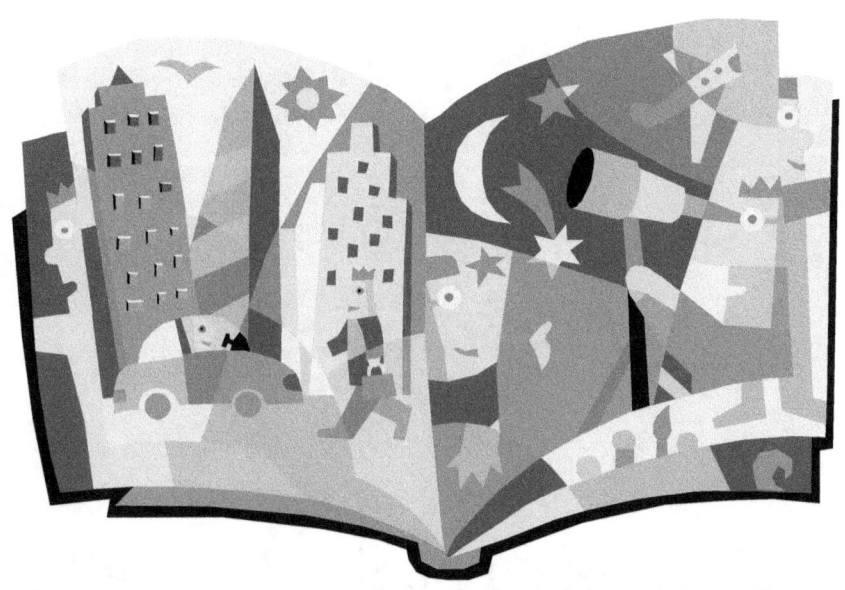

These classical paintings all tell a thousand words, don't you think?

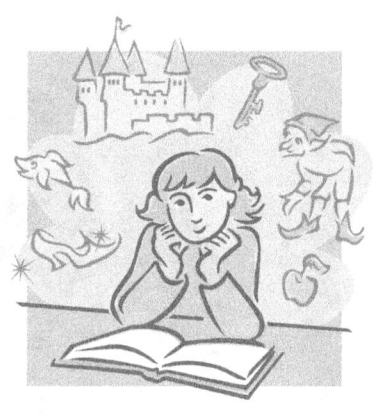

Just like a book, they tell a story too, don't they?

For example, Ellen Grace Parke's painting of children enjoying their art teacher tells many stories. Notice how they dressed with hats, smocks, and suspenders. What else do you see in the painting?

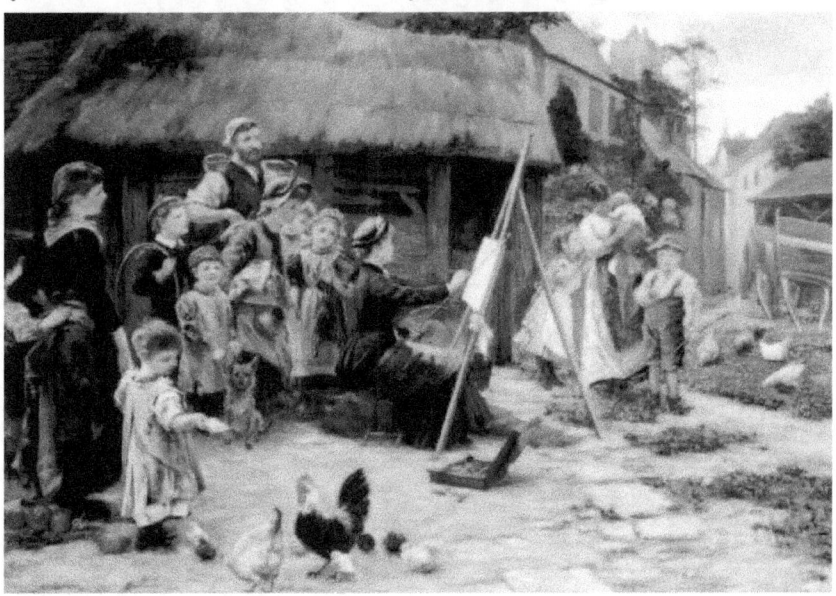

Two Blue Balloons, One Gray by Louise Scott shows three girls in red dresses with balloons and one boy watching them.

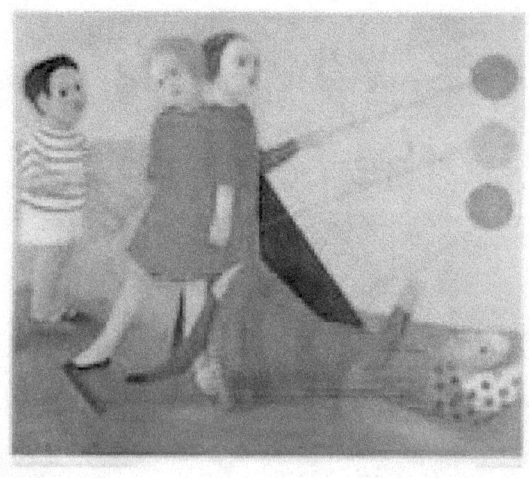

What does this tell you?

Do you think the boy is littler than the girls? I do too because of his clothes and the way he wants a balloon too. Maybe he is their brother.

Mary Cassatt painted
sisters in the painting
called Le Soeurs. It is
called The Two Sisters,also.

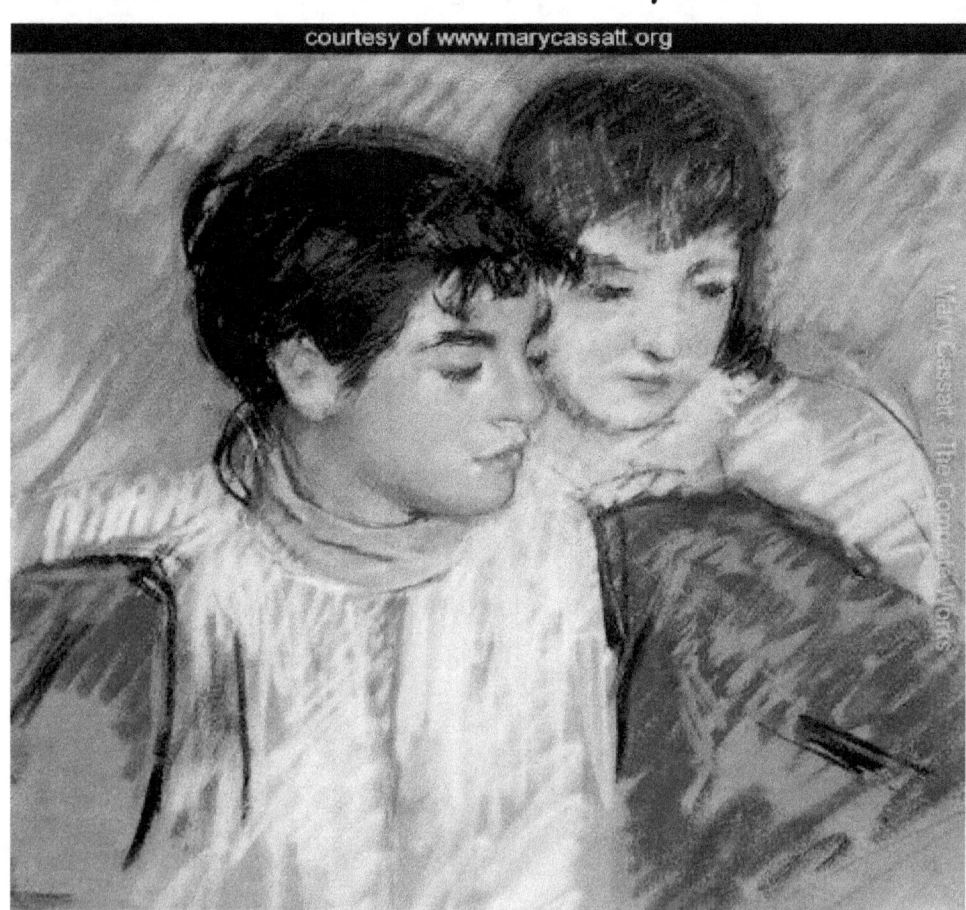

Mary Cassatt did many different pieces of art involving children and women with children.

She used different artistic mediums as well. She used oil paints, pastels and even pencils.

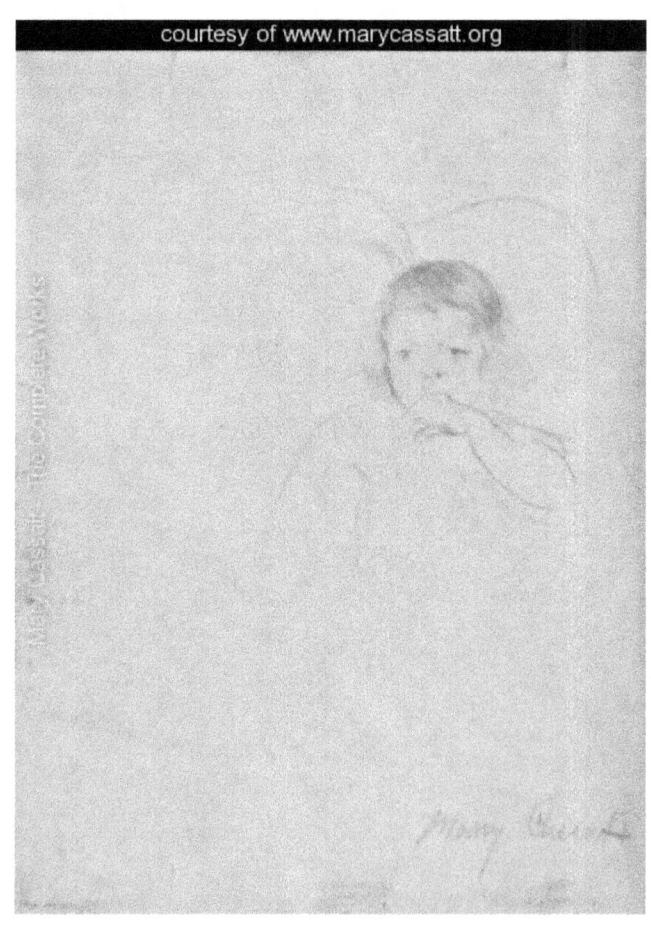

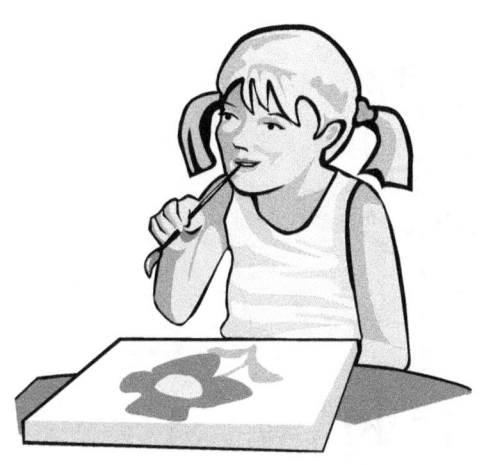

Like Mary Cassatt did, I think you should try all kinds of artistic mediums to find what you like to do and what you are good at doing too.

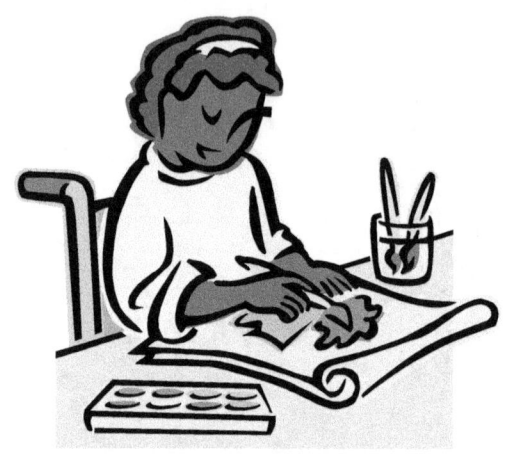

Getting to know
different types of art
helps you feel more
creative when you
experiment with your
talents.

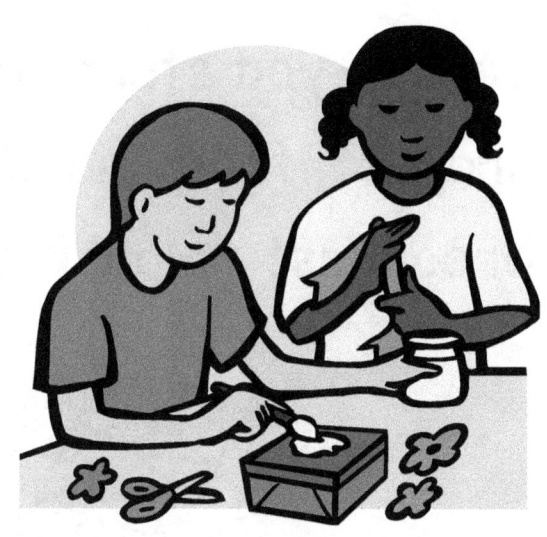

Today let's try working
paints.

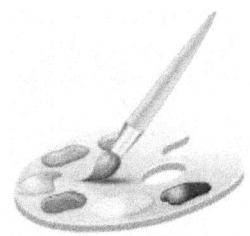

Before you start any project, from making breakfast to packing a

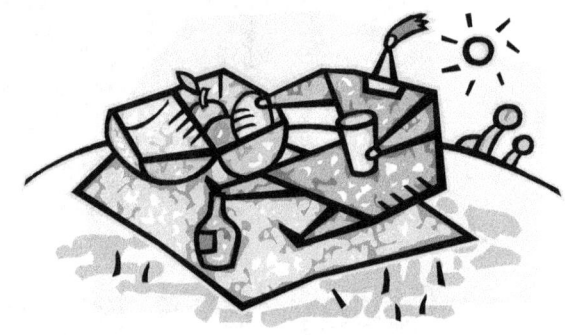

picnic,

make sure you have all of the supplies you need before you start.

You will need :

To wear old clothes,

Put down newspaper

,

Get a few pieces of paper

paint of your choice and a

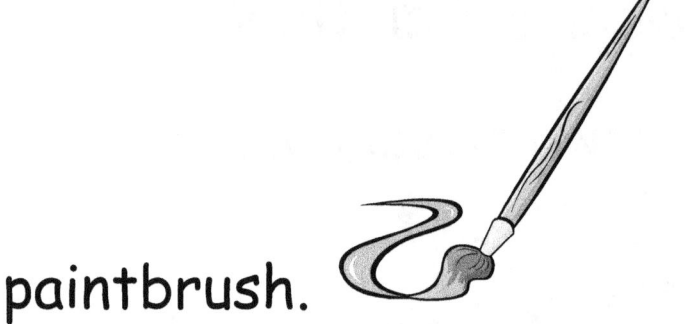

paintbrush.

Watercolor spreads like crazy so experiment on a scratch piece of paper if you decide to use watercolors.

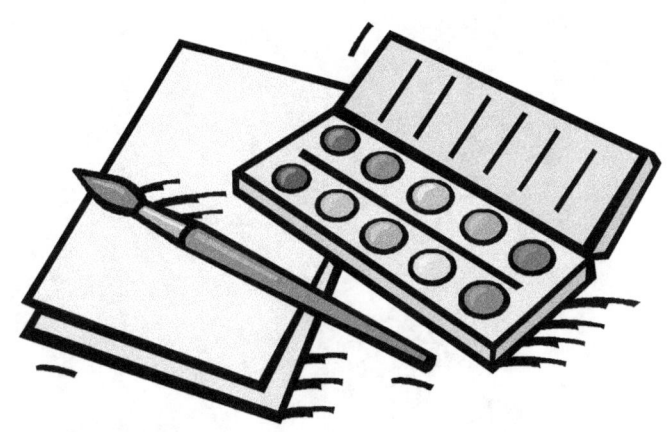

Since you are reading this book, I bet you enjoy books, don't you?

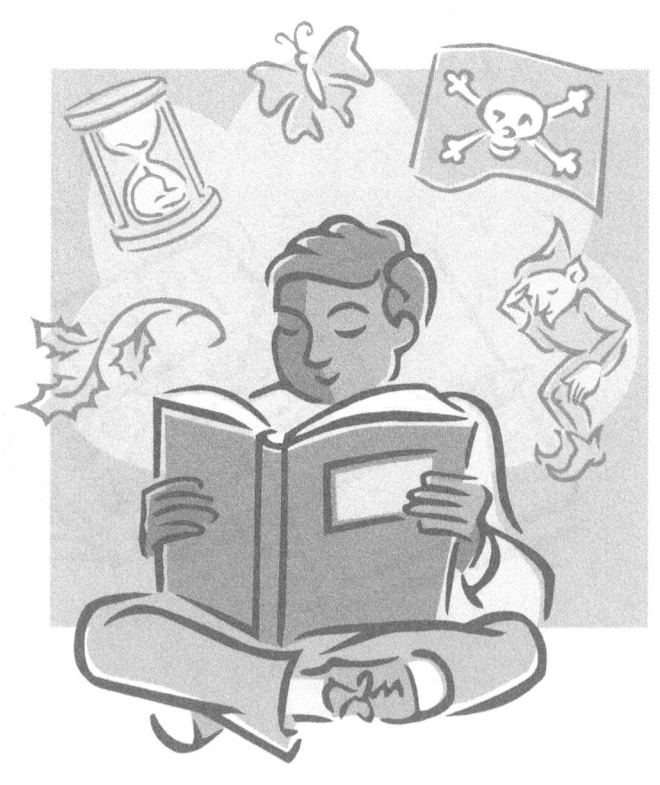

Let's draw a picture that
tells a story about you
reading a book.

Do you like to read alone

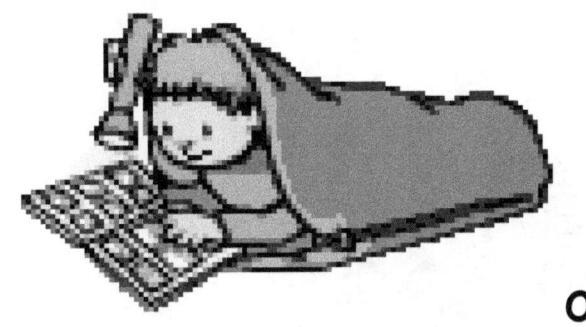

or does

someone read to you?

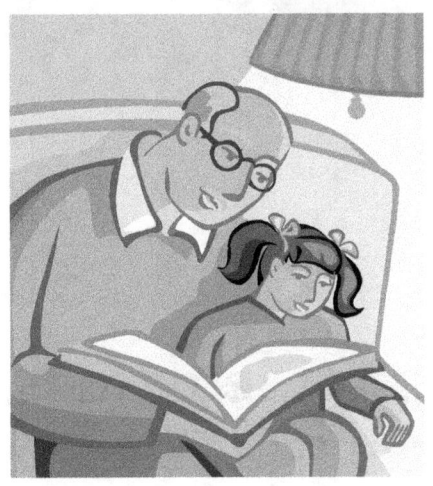

Do you have a favorite
chair or spot where you like
to read?

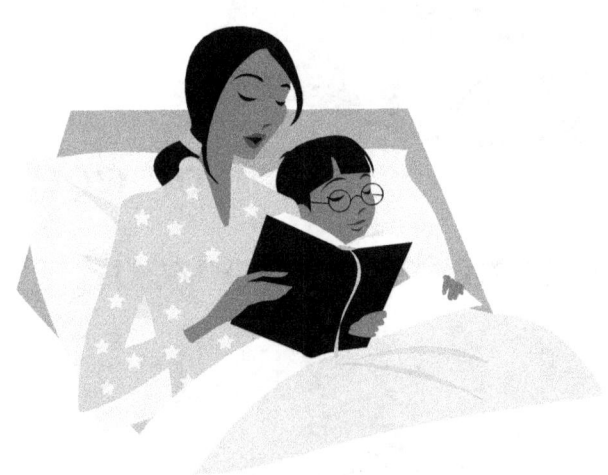

Include these details.

When you finish your work of art, include it in your artist's portfolio!

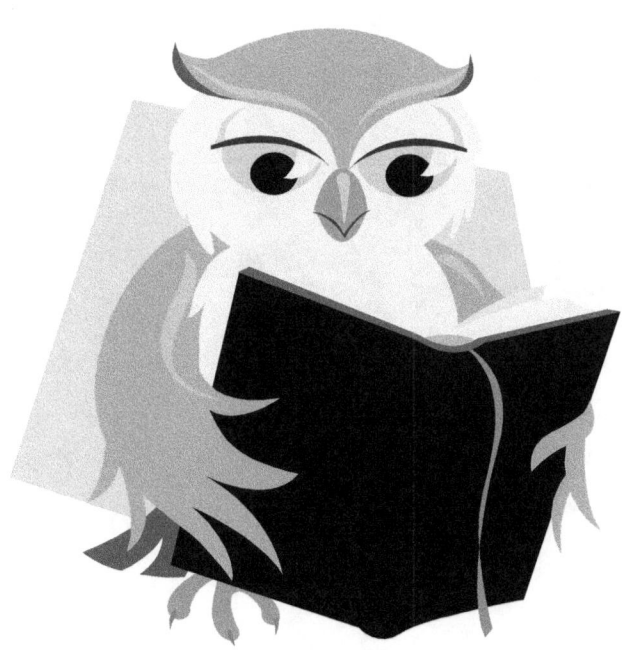

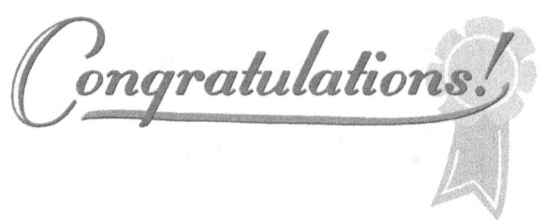

Congratulations!

on such good work!

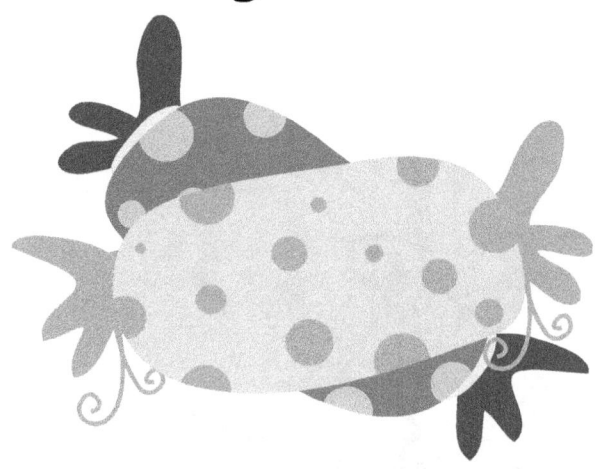